JOURNAL JUMPSTARTS

◆ ◆ ◆ ◆ ◆

Quick Topics and Tips
for Journal Writing

PATRICIA WOODWARD

Cottonwood Press, Inc.
Fort Collins, Colorado

Cottonwood Press, Inc.
107 Cameron Drive
Fort Collins, CO 80525
800-864-4297

ISBN 1-877673-15-3
Printed in the United States of America

Cover design by Patricia Howard

To all those teachers who have given *me*
ideas over the years, with thanks.

INTRODUCTION

◆◆◆◆◆

Journals, daybooks, writer's notebooks — by whatever name you call them, aren't they an enormous amount of work? Are they really worth it?

In a word, yes. Whether your students keep personal journals, subject-related journals or introspective, reactive journals, whether they use three-ring or spiral notebooks, old-fashioned paper or new-fangled word processors, the act of recording their reactions, thoughts, ideas, fears, doubts, dreams, convictions, goals and observations is one of the most ful-filling and meaningful educational activities that they can experience.

Writers know that the very act of writing helps them to clarify their thinking — in fact, to discover what they know. As teachers of writing, we nearly always advise beginning writers to write about something they know — their surroundings, events in their world, themselves. We tell them to observe, to really see even the most minute and mundane aspects of their everyday lives. We encourage them to explore the realm of ideas as well as the physical world. The journal is the ideal vehicle for such ob-servation and exploration.

Keeping a journal is a long-standing literary tradition of people from all walks of life. Because it involves the emotions, it is an activity that will have immediate value and long-lasting meaning for your students. Most of them will do their best writing (fresh, honest and powerful) as they ex-plore their ideas in a risk-free setting. Journal writing will give your stu-dents the opportunity to record their own thoughts, observations, concerns and desires without fear of being judged or graded. Though many may reveal their most personal lives, a journal is not a place for students to bare their innermost secrets, as a diary might be. A journal is, rather, an opportunity for them to look at themselves and their world more thoughtfully and carefully.

Despite its benefits, many teachers approach the idea of journal-writing with concern, if not outright fear. If you are one of those teachers, relax. Journal writing should not be an intimidating experience for either you or your students. This booklet contains suggestions gleaned from over 20 years of having junior high and high school students keep journals. It is designed to help both the teacher and the student overcome some potential roadblocks to successful journaling.

Feel free to use whatever suggestions you think might be helpful, to change the wording if you think of a better way to phrase an idea, to ignore topics that don't seem to "fit." Whatever you do, I hope the experience of student journal writing is as exciting and rewarding for you and your students as it has always been for me and mine.

Patricia Woodward

COMMON-SENSE SUGGESTIONS FOR THE CONCERNS TEACHERS MOST OFTEN EXPRESS ABOUT USING JOURNAL WRITING WITH TEENAGERS . . .

WHY SHOULD I ASK MY STUDENTS TO KEEP A JOURNAL?

Because journals have such personal significance, the benefits of journal-writing are numerous. Your students will experience:

- improved thinking skills

- enjoyment in writing

- involvement in personally meaningful topics

- more dynamic and powerful writing.

One of the greatest benefits of the journal is that it gives a teacher the opportunity to give students individual, personalized attention. With classes of 30 students in 45-minute periods, we have all of about one and a half minutes to spend per student per day. That's not much time to focus on the needs of individual students, let alone time to actually get into personal conversations with each of them. The classroom journal provides that time. Dialogue with students through their journals opens up communication in a way that no other vehicle does.

Who should read the students' journals?

Because you have assigned the journal, you will be expected to read it, but only the student should have the right to allow anyone else to see it, under normal circumstances. Students may ask friends, parents, counselors and classmates to read certain entries, but because of the personal nature of journals, most young people will share them only with people they really trust. As the students learn to trust your acceptance of their writing, you will see their entries become more detailed and dynamic, and your communication with them will be dramatically enhanced.

Your expectations for journals will be quite different from any other type of assigned writing. Encourage students to play with ideas and with words, to write poems, to even occasionally draw pictures if they want to. The more they explore and experiment, the better. To focus on errors will only stifle the flow.

Consequently, you will not want to mark errors in journals but will instead want to encourage clear expression. Ask students to dig for ideas, and comment to ask for clarification or further exploration, but resist the temptation to "correct" them. If you are fortunate enough to have teacher aides or graders, do not have them help you with journals. For you to allow anyone else to read them while they are in your possession would violate the confidential nature of the journals.

How should I handle confidential information?

Frequently, students will share very confidential information about themselves. You may read not only about their private whimsies, but also about their personal tragedies. This is not, however, the time for you to become a therapist. Every teacher is by definition part counselor, but most of us have professional counselors on staff. I tell my students — before they ever begin writing — that I will never share their journals with anyone else without their knowledge (notice that I did not say "permission") and that I will do so only if they are in danger. I tell them that if I learn, for example, that one of them has been a victim of abuse or is threatening suicide, I will immediately ask that young person to go with me to the counselor to get help. I stress that my position requires that I do so and, more importantly, my concern for them demands it.

At the same time, we must also guard against invading the students' privacy. Students can be encouraged to write personally and honestly without being pressured to reveal their most private lives. A diary is more appropriate for entries of that nature. Nevertheless, students will, whether deliberately or inadvertently, make us privy to some very personal and confidential information, and we need to be prepared to respond — both lovingly and professionally.

How should I comment?

The most important rule for commenting in students' journals is that you be honest and that you reply directly to them. This is probably the most time-consuming aspect — not the reading so much as the commenting. However, it is the most important aspect. Nothing encourages students to write more than knowing that someone cares about what they have to say and will write back. (Think about the unbelievable care they take with notes to each other — nearly always ending with that directive: "Write back.")

It is easiest to comment quickly in the margins or at the end of the students' entries, as you read. The comments will typically be brief and positive, encouraging the students, challenging their thinking or asking for clarification. Don't attempt to comment after every entry, but responding periodically gives you the opportunity to establish that very important dialogue with your students. Many teachers try to make at least one positive comment every time a student's journal is turned in. The comments needn't be lengthy, but students do appreciate frequent, direct feedback. (Use any color except red — the psychological response to red ink for most people is to see it as a correction.)

HOW SHOULD I GIVE CREDIT?

Even though you will not be correcting or marking the journals for grades, giving credit for student effort is still essential. Students need to know that you take their journal writing seriously — that you "count" it. Probably the best way to do this *is* to count it.

Have the students date each entry. Ask them to skip a line at the end of an entry, record the new date, and continue writing to the end of each page, rather than starting a new day on a new page. Count the pages, giving a specific number of points for each page. (Ten points per page works well for me.)

Yes, some students will suddenly develop huge penmanship, and others will insist that their pages are much longer than the person's sitting next to them. That's no problem: the teacher gets to decide what constitutes a page. If a student writes three lines to the page, it might take six or seven pages to equal a "normal" page; however, for one who has very tiny penmanship, one page might be counted as two. Feel free to give extra points for exceptionally fine entries. ("This is such a thoughtful observation, it's worth double points!")

The teacher always has the final say in determining the acquired points, so you must be especially clear in establishing the minimum required for a given time period. Depending on the age, ability level, time devoted to writing in class and required out-of-class entries, three to five pages a week is probably sufficient.

On the other hand, it is crucial that neither you nor the students become overly concerned with measuring pages. I tell my students that I will "eyeball" the page and decide if it looks like enough to me. I do my best to be consistent, but if a student thinks I have miscounted, we will re-count the pages together. (Here is where it pays to be flexible without being a push-over.) At the end of each counting period, I record the number in ink and circle it. That way, it is easy to know where to start counting the next time I read.

By the way, some students will become so enamored with their journals that they will write many, many extra pages. I will allow a journal to raise a student's grade only one full grade, and the extra points count only if all required work is in. However, I will not accept lots of extra pages written the night before grades are due. In order to show real progress and growth, journals should be written over an extended period of time, not all at once.

How can I keep up with the reading?

You can handle the work load of reading journals in several different ways:

◆ Have only one or two classes keep journals at the same time.

◆ Have students write regularly, but occasionally take a break. One class might write for a month and then another class write for the next month.

◆ Allow students to turn in their journals as frequently as they like, with the understanding that you will return them as promptly as possible. That way students won't feel they have to wait for an immediate reply when they need one.

◆ Alternate due dates for groups of students. Have one class (or one row) turn their journals in on Mondays, another on Tuesdays, etc.

◆ Be sure students turn in their journals frequently (at least once every two weeks) so that your reading doesn't pile up.

◆ Have students star — or otherwise indicate — entries they particularly want you to read. Then you can quickly read the other entries and focus on the ones that are more important to them.

SHOULD I HAVE RULES ABOUT WHAT THEY WRITE?

Subject matter is another area where you must be somewhat flexible. Sometimes students will do a little testing and write meaningless nonsense, copy lengthy passages from newspapers or magazines or even try to shock you. Typically, if you don't over-react, they will soon stop, if only because they just get tired of it. I sometimes point out that the journal is theirs and ask, "Is this what you want it to say about you?" (True, with some more re-calcitrant students, this approach is not always terribly effective.)

Nevertheless, students should be allowed — even encouraged — to express themselves freely, but within the confines of good taste and acceptability. A guideline I use is that the language should be acceptable to the general public: would the local newspaper use similar language? Students should be reassured that their writing will not be judged on mechanics, but will be evaluated for its content. This doesn't mean that they can't say what they want, but that they should not be offensive in the process.

Spend some time discussing acceptable langauge, but don't give the subject inordinate attention. If offensive language becomes a problem with any student, establish the consequences of breaking the "rule of acceptability." Most schools have fairly clear standards of behavior and acceptable language in class, and these journals, because they are class assignments, are subject to the same expectations. Students rarely violate the standards in their journals, but if they do, deal with them on an individual basis.

HOW CAN I MOTIVATE MY STUDENTS TO WANT TO KEEP A JOURNAL?

Some students may initially resist the idea of journal writing, mainly because they typically resist anything new. However, if you are enthusiastic about the journal and believe in the benefits of keeping such a record of one's intellectual life, your students will eventually come to appreciate its value. Be careful to explain why you think such an activity is worthwhile, and allay their fears by answering their questions before you ask them to begin writing.

Giving them time to write in class is time well spent. Many students become so involved with their in-class writing that they will take the time to finish an entry at home, but for others this may be the only quiet time they have all day. Ten minutes of journal writing at the beginning of class gives students a chance to focus and center. It gives the teacher that same chance.

The choice is not whether to write, but what to write. At first, students' writing may be mundane and superficial, but as they become increasingly involved, they will begin to deal more and more with ideas, rather than just talking about people or relating events. I tell my students that what happens is not nearly as important as their reactions to what happens. You may have to walk around and write questions in the margins of some notebooks to give further prodding, but writing such prompts instead of speaking them has double benefits: the room remains silent and the concentration of others is not broken; plus, the very act of *your* writing promotes *their* writing.

How can I deal with complaints?

Students may complain about any number of things at first, but if you keep your perspective, your sense of humor and your conviction that journal writing is a valuable use of instructional time, you will soon win them over. When students forget to bring their journals, just tell them to use a sheet of notebook paper and add it later. When they whine that they don't have a pen, tell them to borrow one (from you, if necessary). When they claim they can't think of anything to say, tell them to write a note to someone — maybe even to you — and then add it to their journal. If they have complaints about other aspects of keeping their journals, have them put their concerns in writing, and then be sure to address their concerns when you comment. The important thing is to keep them writing. Never allow them to just sit. (This is where your creativity gets a workout!) Try to work out solutions with individual students by really listening to what they are saying and helping them overcome their blocks.

Parents may occasionally wonder about why you don't grade journals, but once they understand the purpose, they are usually very supportive. They just need to be reassured that you provide plenty of opportunity elsewhere for composition writing, editing and revision.

Your own family and/or friends may object at first to the added workload for you, but once you get the hang of rotating the collection, reading for major ideas instead of word-for-word and commenting succinctly, you will not feel quite so overworked and underpaid, and you *will* have time for a social life!

WHERE WILL STUDENTS GET IDEAS FOR THEIR JOURNALS?

Ideally, students will come up with their own ideas for journal topics, but occasionally even the most articulate writers draw a blank. Just as cars sometimes won't start on cold days because of temporarily "dead" batteries, sometimes students can't get going either. When students can't come up with an idea of their own, it is helpful to have one written on the chalkboard or on an overhead projection screen at the front of the room. I call these ideas "journal jumpstarts for the temporarily brain-stalled." If they are truly stalled, students may opt to write on the suggested topic.

On the next pages is a compilation of ideas which have elicited wonderful responses (some more wonderful than others!) from my students over the years, as well as from the students of other teachers with whom I have shared the ideas. Not every suggestion will inspire every student, but there are ideas that should appeal to a wide range of students who need help. Feel free to photocopy the ideas for overhead transparencies. I find that it helps to have at least one idea on the overhead screen each day, for every day there is bound to be someone who needs a "jumpstart" for writing.

(Note: Pages 20-21 provide a brief summary of the importance of journal writing. They are designed for you to photocopy and pass out to your students.)

WHY KEEP A JOURNAL?

- ◆ **for creative expression**
- ◆ **for healthy introspection**
- ◆ **for posterity**
- ◆ **for fun**

Keeping a journal can be one of the most satisfying things you ever do for yourself. A journal is different from a diary in that it need not be kept every day (though most people find that, like exercise, the more consistent they are with it, the more they benefit). With a journal, the emphasis is less on *what* happens each day and more on your *reaction* to what happens. It is a place for you to dream, philosophize, imagine, vent and figure things out. A journal is personal and private and a place where you can get to know yourself better. It is a way for you to chronicle your life's journey — hence, the term "journal."

Sometimes the most difficult step in either a journey or in writing is getting started. The suggested topics in class each day are intended, not to restrict your writing, but to help you begin, if you need a boost. Feel free to ignore the suggestions whenever you have something else you would rather write about. Whether you want to pursue a suggested topic or go off on another tangent, let your own mind be your true guide.

The primary rule for keeping a journal is that you write honestly. Record your observations, work out your worries, indulge your ideas, follow your fancy and *write, write, write!*

HINTS FOR THE BEGINNING JOURNALIST:

♦ Date each entry, including the year. Someday you will want to know when you were thinking these thoughts.

♦ Write in ink. It is more permanent and easier to read later.

♦ Keep your mind on the here and now, not on some future reader.

♦ Say what you really want to say. Don't worry about whether it will sound right to someone else.

♦ Focus on your ideas, your thoughts, your feelings, your observations — not just on external events.

HAPPY JOURNALING!

TRIED AND TRUE TOPICS
TO HELP STUDENTS WHEN THEY
HAVE TROUBLE GETTING STARTED . . .

Who are you — really?

What is the greatest lesson you have ever learned?

Describe yourself as a stranger might see you.

Describe yourself as your best friend knows you.

What are the qualities a best friend must possess?

Describe the qualities you most admire in someone you might call a *hero*.

What makes you special?

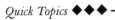

Describe your room from your mom's perspective.

Describe your favorite relative.

Describe the perfect girl/boy.

Describe your favorite place to be alone.

Describe your perfect day.

Write about an unusual dream.

How do people know when you are upset?

List your pet peeves.

What was the most memorable part of your first day of school? Explain.

Will Rogers said, "Everybody is ignorant, only on different subjects." What can you learn from others? What can others learn from you?

What qualities do you really hate in a teacher (no names, please!)?

Describe your favorite teacher.

Describe the ideal job for a teenager.

Compare your life with the growing-up years of one of your parents.

Who has it easier — girls or guys? Defend your position.

When have you been wrongly accused? Explain.

Why should people recycle?

Describe a time when you were afraid.

Describe a time when you were lonely.

Describe a time when you were embarrassed.

Write a letter to a future teenager — one who will be your age now in 100 years.

Write a letter to a long-lost relative or friend, describing your life today.

Write about a time a parent (or another adult) embarrassed you.

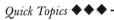

Oscar Wilde said, "Experience is the name everyone gives to their mistakes." What have you learned from "experience"?

Tell about a lie you wish you had not told (or one you are glad you told).

What do you think about people who spread gossip?

What must a person do to be trusted?

When you look in the mirror, what do you see? Go into detail.

Describe the first time you —

- ◆ tried to ski.

- ◆ rode a bike.

- ◆ ice skated.

- ◆ tried to swim.

- ◆ were left alone.

- ◆ had a job.

- ◆ drove a car.

- ◆ ate in a fancy restaurant.

- ◆ got in trouble with a teacher.

- ◆ had a fight with a friend.

- ◆ went on a date.

If you could live anywhere in the world, where would it be? Why?

What question really bothers you?

If you could go to another planet, would you? Explain.

What makes people popular?

What famous person would you most like to meet? Why?

Compare yourself to your favorite animal.

Do you think you have the characteristics associated with your astrological sign? Be specific.

If you had to flee from your burning house, what would you want to save? Explain your choices.

Describe an odd character in your life.

What compliment have you received lately? How did it make you feel?

What causes loneliness?

How important is religion in your life?

Under what circumstances would it be okay to lie?

What do you think causes prejudice?

If you could design the perfect school, what would it be like?

What makes TV worth watching? Not worth watching?

Describe the "coolest" elderly person you know.

Could you be President of the United States? Why or why not?

How are you not the way you seem?

What do you like to do when you are alone?

What kind of parent will you be?

What rules do you think teenagers should have at home?

If you were teacher for a day, what changes would you make? What would you leave the same?

If today were the last day of your life, how would you want to spend it?

If you could change the world, what would you start with?

Describe your worst enemy. (It may not be a person!)

In your family, are you the leader, clown, servant, trouble-maker, peace-maker or what?

Write a letter you would never send.

Who or what makes you laugh?

Write about your strengths. Don't be modest.

Tell about the "coolest" adult you have ever known.

Is it better to be the oldest child, the youngest child, the middle child or an only child? Why?

Do you ever pretend to be something you are not? Why?

Describe your earliest memory. What does that memory say about you or about your life?

Why do people wear masks?

If you could be anywhere else, where would that be?

Are you worried about becoming an adult? Why or why not?

Do you believe in miracles? Why or why not?

Should everyone have responsibilities? Why or why not?

The thing that drives you crazy —

◆ about teachers is . . .

◆ about boys/girls is . . .

◆ about TV commercials is . . .

◆ about joggers is . . .

◆ about _____ is . . .

Henry David Thoreau said, "Things do not change; we change." What do you think he meant?

What TV show ought to be taken off the air? Why?

Do you believe that there is any significance to dreams? Explain.

What is the greatest invention of all time?

Describe an idea for a great invention of your own.

Someone once said, "Whatever does not destroy me makes me strong." What in your life is making you strong?

What do you want to do that you are not allowed to do? *Should* you be allowed to do it?

What is the most effective form of punishment that parents can use in disciplining their children?

Should little kids be allowed to get dirty? Why or why not?

In the song "Ruby Tuesday," the Rolling Stones said, " . . . yesterday don't matter if it's gone —" When should we let our yesterdays go?

Describe your (or someone else's) pet's personality.

What is the best movie you have ever seen? Why is it the best?

What does freedom mean to you?

Some people swear that they have seen unidentified flying objects. Are they crazy?

What effect does the weather have on your mood?

Explain why you listen to your kind of music.

Pretend that you are ruler of the world. What would you do with all that power?

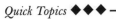

What do you think is the most serious issue facing people today?

What is the most meaningful conversation you have had lately?

Should old people be forced to go to nursing homes?

According to Thomas Dewar, "Minds are like parachutes: they only function when open." Why is it so hard to keep an open mind on some subjects?

What advice would you give someone just beginning

_____?

Do you believe in the supernatural? (Ghosts, perhaps, or ESP?) Why or why not?

What would you do if you saw a ghost?

Do events happen by accident, or is there a plan devised by a supreme being?

Why shouldn't parents try to pick their children's friends?

Defend your opinion on whether or not we should use capital punishment to punish criminals.

Do you believe in marriage? Why or why not?

Why do so many marriages end in divorce?

What is your greatest hope (or fear) for the future?

List ten ways you could improve yourself.

Is it better to be poor but happy or rich but miserable?

Do people have a responsibility to take care of each other?

Do you believe that intelligent life exists on other planets?
What makes you think so?

What famous person has touched your life in some way? Did you see or meet the person? Is the person a relative? Did the person affect your life in some other way?

How do clothes influence our behavior?

What characteristic about the opposite sex annoys you the most?

Why do you think people gossip?

Describe the perfect parent.

When you get your feelings hurt, how do you respond?

What do you wish you could do something about? Explain.

According to a Japanese proverb, "Words are the root of all evil." Do you agree or disagree? Why?

If you could visit any part of the world, where would you go first?

Why should people be careful about what they say?

Describe your own personal "ten commandments."

Describe the perfect job for you.

What would you do if a good friend repeated a secret you had told him or her?

Why is it a good idea to treat everyone with courtesy?

What is the biggest time-waster in your life?

Paint a picture with words of the face of —

♦ someone you love

♦ the oldest person you know

♦ your best friend

♦ the most unusual person you have seen

♦ yourself

Should children be forced to receive a religious education? Explain.

Do you have plenty of time to do what you want to do? Explain.

Describe when you feel most in tune with nature.

What are you thankful for today?

Describe the best gift you have ever received.

Describe the best gift you have ever given.

What kind of future life do you imagine for yourself?
What will you have to do to make it come true?

What is your favorite daydream?

If you could live in another time in our history, when
would it be? Why?

What one thing have you always wanted to tell someone
you know?

Why do some people find fault with every little thing?

What do people have to do to have friends?

What is something you do to help —

  ◆ your friends?

  ◆ your family?

  ◆ yourself?

  ◆ the world?

Recount your weirdest dream.

Describe your favorite outfit (clothes). Why do you like it so much?

How have you changed in the last year?

If you had a friend who was in serious trouble, what would you do?

Which do you think is more harmful to young television viewers, violence or nudity? Why?

Describe your favorite time of day.

Tell about a time when you did something that took a lot of courage for you. (Examples: learning to swim, giving a speech, asking for a date, having surgery, standing up for yourself, etc.)

What is something important you have learned, something that did not come out of a book?

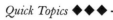

What can we do to eliminate homelessness?

Who should be responsible for providing sex education — parents, teachers or religious leaders? Why?

Define *peer pressure.*

Describe your most memorable holiday, from start to finish. Recall the food, smells, gifts, decorations, relatives, traditions, unusual events, etc.

Describe your favorite places to play when you were a child.

Why do you think people abuse drugs?

Have you created a "masterpiece" yet in your life? It could be concrete or abstract. Describe it.

According to Rene Descartes, "It is not enough to have a good mind; the main thing is to use it well." Is it better to be average and use all you have, or to be smart and use half of what you have?

Describe one act for which you would like to be remembered.

Describe a characteristic, talent or tendency you have inherited.

What about your life is heroic or admirable?

Are you anybody's hero? Explain.

What advice would you give to a man or a woman about to become a stepparent?

Do all animals have the right to live? How about insects? Why or why not?

Which would you rather be, beautiful or brainy? Why?

How can you turn a failure into something positive?

What do you value that you could offer as a gift to someone you love?

What makes people want to join gangs?

If you had to lose one of your senses, which one would be the last one you would pick? Why?

Invent a "magic machine" and describe it.

If you were to suddenly lose your sight, what three things would you miss seeing the most?

How would you describe music to someone who can't hear?

What is the most delightful thing you have ever seen? Describe it.

Can someone who is not intelligent teach other people something? Explain.

Is there a relationship between being intelligent and being a good person? Explain.

What is the worst advice you have ever received? The best?

If you could have an operation that would make you twice as intelligent as you are, would you have it? Why or why not?

Describe a classmate or teacher who will stand out in your memory 20 years from now.

Describe a group that you would feel comfortable joining.

Imagine that you suddenly have to go into hiding. Describe who would hide with you, what few belongings you would take and where you would hide.

In what area of your life are you walking when you should be running? What can you do to get yourself to run?

Should friends offer advice to each other in matters of the heart? Explain.

In your family, who gives the best advice? Why do you think so?

Who, among your friends or family, understands you the best? What makes you think so?

If you could make the rules for this class (or this school, or the world), what would they be? Explain why you think the rules would be necessary.

Should friends date each other? Defend your position.

What proof do you have of your existence?

Briefly describe the best book you have ever read. Why does it appeal to you so much?

If these walls (pick any walls) could talk, what stories would they tell?

Do plants have feelings? Emotions? Personalities? How about animals?

Is there any such thing as innocence?

Why do good people have to suffer sometimes?

In what situations is it good for a person to cry?

Does equality of the sexes really exist?

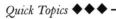

Are all people really created equal?

Is there life after death?

Considering what you know now, what would you have done differently in your life?

What does the saying "Opportunity only knocks once" mean?

How can parents influence their children's choices? Think about friends, religion, college, hobbies, careers, spouses, etc.

Do you think you will marry someday or remain single? Why?

Do you view the future with fear or optimism? Explain.

Why is honesty the best policy?

How important is one's reputation?

Should all people participate in some kind of sport?

When should people control their emotions? When should they let them show?

s wrong with —

- ◆ smoking?

- ◆ using drugs?

- ◆ pre-marital sex?

- ◆ swearing?

- ◆ stealing?

- ◆ copying your friend's homework?

- ◆ *R* or *X*-rated movies?

- ◆ pornography?

- ◆ dumping trash wherever you want?

What is wrong with —

- ◆ pretending that you like someone or something?

- ◆ flattery?

- ◆ telling white lies?

- ◆ hunting?

- ◆ gambling?

- ◆ wearing make-up?

- ◆ parties?

- ◆ being lazy?

- ◆ being competitive?

What do the terms *pro-choice* and *pro-life* mean to you?

What does it mean to truly be an individual?

Should America become involved in other countries' wars? Explain.

Is there such a thing as an honest politician?

What do you think your mom was like when she was your age?

What do you think your dad was like when he was your age?

Copyright 1996 © Cottonwood Press, Inc. • 305 West Magnolia, Suite 398 • Fort Collins, Colorado 80521

Describe the perfect —

- ◆ house.

- ◆ sport.

- ◆ hideaway.

- ◆ friend.

- ◆ boss.

- ◆ principal.

- ◆ parent.

- ◆ teacher.

- ◆ pet.

- ◆ date.

Should students be forced to make career choices at an early age? Why or why not?

Can money buy happiness? Explain.

Can you imagine living the way your grandmother or grandfather did? Why or why not?

What will your grandchildren say about you someday?

What does it mean to "act your age"? Should people act their age at all times?

What is one of the nicest things someone has ever done for you?

What is the best way to meet new people?

What acts of kindness have you performed lately?

What do you think about the trend toward requiring students to wear uniforms?

Explain the saying *Carpe diem*, or "Seize the day."

What's the weirdest thing that ever happened to you?

How do you get your own way?

What would be your "most excellent adventure"?

Explain your concept of "heaven" or "paradise."

What jobs (responsibilities, chores, obligations) should teenagers have?

How do you practice self-discipline?

Do parents have unreasonable expectations of their children today? Explain.

What is the worst habit you have? Why don't you break it?

Describe your favorite performer.

Should teenagers have allowances? Explain your thoughts.

Should teenagers have cars? Explain your position.

What responsibilities are part of being sexually active?

What qualities must a person have to be a good leader?

What should you do to be a better person?

Explain whether or not you think it is ever okay to —

- ◆ lie to spare someone's feelings.

- ◆ steal food if you are hungry.

- ◆ kill an innocent living thing.

- ◆ cheat on your girlfriend/boyfriend.

- ◆ be disrespectful to an adult.

- ◆ cut down a friend.

- ◆ be mean to a disabled person.

- ◆ keep a valuable, lost item that you find.

- ◆ break a promise.

- ◆ deliberately disobey a parent, teacher or other authority.

- ◆ put your life at risk by doing something dangerous.

What do you think about teenagers having babies? Explain.

Explain why you like playing your favorite sport.

Describe who you think is the best athlete in any sport.

What does a person learn by playing sports?

What games would you recommend that all people know how to play?

Do you usually do what you say you are going to do? Why or why not?

Would you rather (explain how your choice shows your personality) —

- ◆ take a hike or work a crossword puzzle?

- ◆ read a book or play a game of basketball?

- ◆ go to a movie or a play?

- ◆ go to a concert or a dance?

- ◆ listen to music or play an instrument?

- ◆ drive a car or ride a motorcycle?

- ◆ swim upstream or float through life?

- ◆ go to college or get a job right out of high school?

- ◆ live alone, with a roommate, in a commune or with a spouse?

Would you rather (explain how your choice shows your personality) —

- ♦ play tennis or football?

- ♦ take a cruise or go camping?

- ♦ walk or jog?

- ♦ eat at a fancy restaurant or go on a picnic?

- ♦ cook your own meals or order a pizza?

- ♦ live in a city or on a farm?

- ♦ wear cutoffs or dress up?

- ♦ take a shower or a bath?

- ♦ sleep late or get up early?

- ♦ have a cat or a dog for a pet? A snake or a rat? A rabbit or a pit bull?

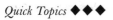

How are you with money? Explain.

What do we owe to other people?

It is your best friend's birthday. Your gift is a memory for every year you two have been friends. Briefly summarize those memories for your friend.

What current fads do you think will become a standard part of our culture?

John Madden, former head coach of the Oakland Raiders, once said, "It doesn't matter if you win or lose — only if you win." Why is winning so important to some people and not others?

Is it true that what you don't know can't hurt you?

Can a person ever work *too* hard at something? Do you?

According to one Zen proverb, "To light a light is to cast a shadow. One cannot exist without the other." What are some contradictions in *your* life? Are they necessary, or not?

Why do people in groups sometimes do things they would not normally do on their own? Have you ever experienced this?

Do you live for the past, the present or the future?

Henry Ford said, "Thinking is the hardest work there is, which is the probable reason why so few engage in it." Do you agree that thinking is the hardest work there is?

How much influence do your friends have over you?

How much influence do you have over your friends?

Write a letter to a famous person. Ask for advice, opinions, explanations. Tell the person why you admire him or her.

Does the world ever seem too complicated? What can you do to simplify your life?

Should you ever question your beliefs? Why or why not?

What are some little things that upset you, even though you know they shouldn't?

Is it better to be a tidy person or a messy person? Why? Which one are you?

When is it good to argue?

In "The Wall, Part II," Pink Floyd sings, "We don't need no education . . . we don't need no thought control . . ." Are education and thought control the same thing? Do schools practice thought control?

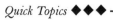

What's the best part about spring?

What's the best part about summer?

What's the best part about fall?

What's the best part about winter?

Oscar Wilde said, "Some cause happiness wherever they go; others whenever they go." Who makes you happy? Why?

What happens when a person has no hope?

Would you rather be an astronaut or a rattlesnake keeper? A surgeon or a concert pianist? A garbage collector or a teacher? Why?

Does complaining do any good?

Is life better for little kids, teenagers, young adults, middle aged or retired people?

Leo Rosten said, "If a picture is worth a thousand words, please paint me the Gettysburg Address." Would you rather use words or pictures to show how you feel or what you think?

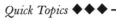

Do you spend your money carefully? How about your time? Your energy?

What has someone done to you that you haven't forgiven? Do you think you ever will? Do you think you ever should?

Philip Wylie once said, "Ignorance is not bliss — it is oblivion." What would happen if a person had no knowledge?

Do you have any friends you wish were your relatives? Do you have any relatives you would choose for friends?

What do you have to do to be in the "in" group?

What must you do today to make your dreams a reality?

Are humans a higher life form than other animals?

Should there be a limit to how long a person can collect welfare money?

Is it okay to gossip about friends? About celebrities?

How can you tell when someone is lying?

Is art worthwhile?

Would you rather read the book or watch the movie? Why?

Should drugs be illegal?

Do you agree that it takes a village to raise a child?

Is it more important to please yourself or others?

Should people have the right to burn the American flag?

Should little boys play with dolls?

Should kids work when they are in school?

Is there any reason not to eat meat?

What is reality?

Should people be allowed to decide when they die?

Is it true that all you need to know about life you learned in kindergarten?

What does the Pledge of Allegiance mean? Consider the words themselves.

Should children be allowed to play with toy guns?

Do you think your life is like a soap opera in any way? Explain.

Should people respect their elders?

Which of these items would be the hardest for you to live without — telephone, television or blowdryer?

Should the Internet be regulated? If so, who should do it?

Should one parent always stay at home with the children?

Do you have a "cause"? If so, what is it?

Should there be a limit to how much time teenagers get to spend on the phone every night?

Do you plan to dye your hair when it turns gray?

Is it important for people to be "up" on current events in the news?

If you were to do volunteer work, what would you do?

Do celebrities have the right to privacy?

Should sports figures behave as though they are role models?

Would you rather take someone's picture or have your own picture taken?

Should students who are disruptive in the classroom be allowed to stay in school?

Is it important to speak more than one language?

Should kids be forced to attend school?

Is affirmative action necessary?

Why do you think we haven't had a female or a minority president? Do you think we ever will?

Should Americans buy only products made in the United States?

Should a woman change her last name when she gets married? Why or why not?

Do you agree or disagree with the idea of "guilt by association"?

Do you think young people are discriminated against?

James Thurber said, "It is better to know some of the questions than to know all the answers." Do you agree?

Do you have your own personal moral code? What is it?

How much homework should students have every night?

What is your favorite kind of weather?

Describe a food you really hate.

How old do you want to be when you die?

What do you have in your life because people pay taxes?

What kind of person do you want to be when you are old?

Should English be the official language of the United States?

If others wouldn't make fun of you for what you wore, what would you wear?

Is it ever okay for parents to open their teenagers' mail, read their diaries or listen in on their phone calls?

How can you tell when someone is smart? Is there a difference between being "street smart" and being "book smart"?

Eleanor Roosevelt said, "Happiness is not a goal, it is a by-product." What do you think she meant?

ABOUT THE AUTHOR

Patricia Woodward is a high school English and drama teacher in Fort Collins, Colorado. She has 31 years of experience and has received many awards and honors in her career, including being named Colorado State Teacher of the Year in 1987. She has received three fellowships from the National Endowment for the Humanities and received a fellowship from the National Council for Basic Education. She is a frequent presenter and consultant for organizations, schools and colleges throughout Colorado.

COTTONWOOD PRESS ORDER FORM

Please send me _____copies of *Journal Jumpstarts.* I am enclosing $7.95 plus shipping and handling ($3.50 for one book, $2.00 for each additional book). Colorado residents add 24¢ sales tax, per book. Total amount _____.

Name _____

School (only if using school address) _____

Address _____ \ _____

City _____State _____ Zip Code _____

Method of Payment:

    ❏ Payment enclosed   ❏ Credit Card   ❏ Purchase Order

Credit Card# _____Expiration Date _____

Signature _____

Send to:

Cottonwood Press, Inc.
107 Cameron Drive
Fort Collins, CO 80525
1-800-864-4297

Call for a free catalog of practical materials for